July 2016.

SESSIONS

Adam & Claire

— I hope that you find
some of the light & noise
in here!

Best wishes
for your kind support.

Love, [signature].

SESSIONS

John J. McKenna

Sessions
Copyright © 2016 John J. McKenna

All rights reserved. Red Dashboard LLC Publishing retains right to reprint. Permission to reprint any poem must be obtained from the author.

ISBN-13: 978-1-970003-00-0

Cover artwork © "Lusting" (2008) by Marissa Woodrow;
Painting property of John J. McKenna—you cannot reuse this artwork without permission from owner and or artist.

Cover Design © Red Dashboard LLC Publications

Published by
Red Dashboard LLC Publishing
Princeton, NJ 08540
www.reddashboard.com

Acknowledgements'

"And Now" and "New Autumn"
appeared in the Spring 2010 and
Autumn/Winter issues of the River Poets
Journal, respectively.

"If sought", "The White Horse (New
Amsterdam on Hudson)", "An account of the
first of Summer's Muse", and, 'Belfast"
appeared in **Vox Poetica** in May 2013,
December 2012, May 2016 and July 2016,
respectively.

And Thank You—

Thank you – for so many, so generous, my
family and friends - should you have not
heard my spoken voice yet say, "thank you."

Additional gratitude, for the heartfelt support
and encouragement of: The River Poets
and editor—Judith Lawrence; vox poetica
and editor, Annmarie Lockhart; The New
Hope Beat Poets; The Buddy Joe Squad;
and the light of Asami.

For Diane Kuenzel—

who first and gently taught
that windows
are meant to be opened,
and remain so

Table of Contents

The New Sessions

Invitation 5
First Light 6
Autumn 8
And Now 11
Blue Dusk 12
New Autumn 14
Each Stone 16
Beneath 18

The LA Sessions

The Gallery
    Part I – Allure 21
    Part II – The Gift 23
    Part III – Sitting Near 25
    Part IV – The Unveiling:
      The Curtain Finally Drawn 27
      The Princess Of New Julfa 32
A Note Found In A
Re-used Prescription Bottle 33
A Short And Timely Reply 34
Epilogue: 708-A 35

The Blue Morning Kitchen Sessions

When, That Time I saw 39
Prophecies Foretold of Her 41
In Wander, Wonder,
  Wait and Worship 44
If Sought 46

Details 47
Desire 49
Indoctrillumination 51
Known Not Sought 54
The Heart Knew First 56
The Bounty 58
And So Begins
  The Folding Down 60
An Account of Her
  Most Recent Visit 63

The East Village Sessions

A Cup Of Coffee, A Cigarette
  And An Attempt To Read
    The Day's Newspaper 69
6 Uptown Summer 71
Summer Downtown #2   72
E. H. Sailing – 1911 73
The White Horse
  (New Amsterdam On Hudson) 76

The Studio Sessions

Why Whisper 81
Why To Have Paused 84
Once a Hummingbird:
  Again A Flower 86
On The Celebration Of Your
  Entrance And Unveiling 87
The Embrace 85
Poem In G Minor 91
Still Life (Now Properly Titled) 94

The North Beach Sessions

The BEAT ………… 97
Who's That With the Horn ………… 99
Did You See Her? ………… 102
Do You Dare? ………… 106
Mid Simmer's Knight Dream ………… 109
Wish Me Something New ………… 111
On Russian Hill ………… 112

The New Sessions

Invitation

I'll be dreaming tonight

you might
you may
just find me there

above the water
barefoot
quick, gliding like Peter

warm wander wink
whistling
like lazy Huck
along the river

poised proper
posture perfect
patient
like young Gatsby still
waiting in the Summer soft-lit gazebo

there
and beneath the willows
in white

First Light

whisper not
She rises
a song of perpetual harmony

calling yes
command to rise alongside Her

    "I wake this day
    radiant, purpose and promise."

from blue night
and wash of rain

    "Rise with me
    see and seize the splendor abundant."

from shore and waking warble of seabird
the skittering busy legs of sandpiper
from break line and beach and again

from drowsy float of river otter
and slow standing posture of new-eyed hill deer

from bounding barn dog breaking bark
and the steady pace of Palomino across azure
    plain
not yet fully illuminated
first light
lifting as mane and muscle shake

to the crooked cross scurry of western beach crab
and the slow majesty beneath this pacing deep
Pacific surf

> "I call to each
> in a voice familiar spoken – in all universal.
>
> This day has come – rise with me, I call you to
> my side to
> grace with me across this moment, this orb
> and Earth.
> Soon it seems that slumber and Sister Moon,
> will tire and tease us back
> to nest and den, hollow and hole.
>
> But for now,
> Dawn and Day and Eternal – this gift"

Autumn

Autumn has again come to the East

burnt orange
pear gold rustle of leaves

softer
gentle
yet certain and more distant
Dawn

She and She again
and again
by natural light

Autumn

long stretching caring fingers
like delicate branches
licked with fading but never
forgotten light

She begins to carefully
gently
lay and fold
Summer down

Earth
still warm in this moment
She reminds all that this too is welcomed and right

this
ever to repeat
kiss of gratitude

   "How brightly you have burned Summer!

Come to me now—
I quiet hush the remaining
cicadas for you
as I always will.

Rest deeply within me—
Reflect.

Find me again—
I have not left you.

Only silent
steady
grace
patience and waiting.

I will hold you to me again
past the bitter Winter.

And it is I
who again will rise.

You will know me
should you care to look
and listen
on brushed blue morning window sills

Not shadow
but steady
subtle illumination
and whisper."

And Now

and now, this day
the gift glow of Spring has sought the West

this deep eve
cool still
not yet hot
this restless turning to Summer's right
has welcomed itself to the settled Earth
reminding that Spring like Gemini is of two songs

stars now whisper and where clouds wandered

and now
this night

Blue Dusk

near night
gray leaning sky
still above a white land
laid to silence

witness and pause
to last light
reflected

new shadows wake
on horizon's line stretching still

Nature's fallen pearls
inviting
at window and door

a path not to find
but make

snow
winks a game
hide and seek
with each new step

slowly and patiently

across this landscape
decorated

the hush whisper white
of new lace
and linen

New Autumn

and so it is
that night
and cicada's call
now to new and slower melody
portent of Fall to follow

it begins again
as Night chorus of crickets
the click-click-reck-reck

pause

Summer's once urgent heat
beginning now to burn light
slightly less brightly
as Her radiant hair lays closer
and sooner still on August horizon

Autumn
She of legend and whisper, tale and fable
songs of her long slow reaching conjure
Her stretch yawn and slumber
begin in hush-whisper-hush

from Dusk and Night and Dawn
to gentle wake and rise
in bush and grass
in bed and meadow
on porch step and window sill

She will as She has always
while they begin again to dream
hint remember and imagine
She will come again to hold and keep

through white Winter's sleep
returning to the face of Nature
as Spring's morning to come

Each Stone

green gray
burnt brown
marble
mauve
and rust

slow grind
beneath
wander
way
and wait

feet
and hoof
and wheel

movement
and pause
reflection
and resumption

these stones
having been laid out
at depth thought sufficient
to cover and hold
our arrival
stay
and soon departure

they too however

scattered and separated
and
in turn
whether cracked kicked
broken busted or buried
surrender as well

Beneath

beneath the scratch
chip paint

dry knuckles
crevice filled

speckled fleck
dusted dotted smeared
white cover of hands
Summer tan still

wrinkles

a life's topography

accented
beneath hot water hot

before folding the
curled corners
of the brittle gray drop cloth

hands

still warm
of work begun

not yet finished

The LA Sessions

The Gallery

Part I – Allure

almond eyes, the color of the Orient
jade charged, gold flecked

high royal cheekbones graced
above her mouth of promise

elegance and ecstasy, this mouth

excruciating in want for and need for
in want of and need of

body
perfect perfumed paradox
fig and cassis

lines
soft and slender

wanting, needing, searching
asking, trembling

whispering,
promising
echoing

evoking

fair, and skin the colour
of white peach linen

Part II – This Gift

this gift and grace
quiet and at peace

this voice, gifted and musical,
this smile, radiant and welcoming
this touch, finger to lip to tongue

elegance made in simple lines
eyes that cast, call and conjure

grace given, gifted without occasion
in life
to life
for life

in moments still
quiet
crowded

she, sitting near
this lady, calm in herself
so graceful in and to this world

her hand slowly reaches
meeting his
she breathes deeply, calmly and content

she speaks to him and leans toward

arms before her, patiently yet flowing in harmony
with her words

the heart
and these thoughts

simple grace as he too breathes

Part III – Sitting Near

I.

her slender fingers to the china
soft brushed with rose

"Will you share the tea?" he asks
"Yes," she responds
smiling

"May I taste the bread?"
"Yes, please." She replies
her eyes to his
a slow blink invitation and acceptance

"May I taste the honey?"
"Yes, yes of course, you must."
herself and warmth

to her he asks
"Will you warm me like the tea?
Will you nourish me like the bread?
Will you gift and treat me like the honey?"

She whispers:
"I have and will warm your soul like the tea.
I have and will warm your heart and hands

I will burn bright
our imagination
together"

"I have and will nourish your soul like the bread.
I have and will nourish your heart and hands

I will rise swiftly
our hope
together."

"I have and will gift and treat your soul like the honey.
I have and will gift and treat your heart and hands

I will give all
our moment
together."

II.

"Will we sing now?"

let our rhythm and cadence come
as we first came to each other

time and unexpected delight

Part IV – The Unveiling:
The Curtain Finally Drawn

the profile, the perfect posture, the cool confidence, the concentration, the glasses, the sandals, the jeans, the Arabian gold drop earrings, the graceful quiet, her magnificent eyes, the modest smile, the soft slow blink of lashes, the gentle acknowledgment and hello.

the "do you mind if I might ask what it is that you are working on?", the "of course not", the easy polite dialogue, "do you mind if I join you at your table?", the "no, please do", the conversation, the invitation, the evening, the swish of the dress, her eyes again – inviting, casting, calling, conjuring all at once – bright twice reflecting and radiant independently from within.

the cheese, the wine, the walk, the hands – soft long elegant fingers and fancy, the grace, eloquence, the thoughtful and proper speech decorated and draped in the warmth of a British accent.

the impromptu picnic at dusk, the sky, the exceptional Spanish wine, the small Greek ceramic cups, the grape leaves, the smile, the quiet look at and look away, the hands crossing – briefly touching, the laughter, her eyes, the hands again finding one another and closing the space between.

her eyes, the mouth, the lips, the high royal
cheekbones, the kiss, the warm hum of the
moment, the mouth again, finger to lip to tongue,
the insatiable mouth, the beauty, the petite figure,
the uninterrupted lines of her body, the gliding hips,
the perfect full summer apple breasts, her eyes –
darker and yet somehow brighter still, the soft flat
pale belly, the soft delicate dark puff of hair above
her gift, the curvature of her waist, the grace of her
beautiful lines, the effortless femininity of her
nakedness, the splendor, the offering, the give, the
glide, the slow touch, the soft mouth, the close pull,
the hum, the moan, the push, the thrust, the pull,
the please, the pleasing, the moan again, the grip,
the take, the hum again – stronger louder rising, the
lift, the sweat, the give and give again, the get and
get again, the grind, the hum to howl, the hard hold,
the release, the collapse, the bodies intertwined,
the breath short panting, the mouth wet, the eyes
illuminating before the drifting sleep, the weight of
her head on my chest as we breathed together.

the allure, the again, the draw, the slight pull, the
tease and take and smirk and giggle, the evocation,
the charm, the mystery, the mystic, the cast, the
conjure, the spell, the languages, the legends, the
lore, the stories and fables and fantasies, the slow
pull, the twist, the turn, the lean in, the lean out, the
giddy girl whirl and spin, the soft touch of your hand
across my shoulder as you stepped behind me in
the kitchen.

the perfect posture in the morning chair at first light
while weeping, the moment that you shared with

me that your Father had died, the haunting vision of beautiful you alone and trembling in a black dress of shiva and sorrow.

the conversations on the kitchen floor, the talk and the listening till near dawn, the cigarettes, the bottles of wine and water, the watching you dry your hair with a towel, the soft voice you used when stating my name, the weekend away, the white wine and balcony, the conversation on the bridge and how you shared and described Armenia, the lamp that would be yours, watching you take a bath and luxuriate in yourself.

telling you that "I was in love with you" for the first time as you boarded a train, your bright illuminating smile and confident stride on the platform as you walked toward me when returning.

the holding, the mouth wet and hot, the twist, the turn, the gasp, the crying, the phone calls, the abrupt speak, the hang ups, the call backs, the ranting, the "I am so sad", the "I am scared", the walking away, the turning away, the eyes – for the first time near unrecognizable, the voicemails, the phone ringing and ringing and ringing, the quick sharp profanity, the tears, the threats, trembling, the "I dreamt of Death last night, He recognized me, He knew my smell and taste and I his", wiry washed out wide-eyed morning look on your face, holding you and rocking you, her eyes – somehow even more fragile than at any point before, the apologies, the twist, the turn, the tightening, the

night you took the pills, "How many?", "Not enough
to stay away, just enough to get away."
knowing still that I was in love with you when I
watched you wear your Grandmother's white dress
at Yiskah's bat mitzvah– the realization then that
you were – to me then – the most beautiful woman
I had ever seen, the asking you to stay.

the move, the hotel, the apartment, the cards, the
care packages, the money, the rent, the co-signing
the lease, the packing, the boxes, the hours
readying you and your things for the move, the
shipping, the unpacking on the west coast, the new
bed, the new book cases the table and chairs, the
boxes, the books, the medical bills, the back taxes,
the wires, the phone calls the phone being off the
hook all night, the quick and cavalier profanity, the
"I need help", the call, the hang ups, the vulgarity,
the common profanity, the adolescent speak of
other men - past, present and future, the "someone
is following me" – hang up, the "I am pregnant" –
three times – hang up.

the trip to Catalina, the white wine, the cheese and
apricot, the necklace that would be yours but never
shine, the superior and condescending tone, the
arrogance, the absence of simple kindness, the
shocking bitterness, the discontent, the dinner, the
hard and harsh slap to my face, the way you stood
slouched crying and banging the back of your head
against the stone wall – the nauseating dull thud of
it, the screaming in the hotel, the scratching, the
violence that you inflicted upon yourself and me

that night, your profile sitting in the tub fully dressed rocking trembling weeping.

the phone calls, the randomness, the erratic voice, the laughter, the crying, the "hold on a minute", the stolen purse, the trouble at work, the trouble with family, the telling my friends and family nothing out of shame – telling the Police everything so that they would hurry and go "Please go, she said that she had readied everything to kill herself, please go I fear", the lies, the sick fuck verb you did to me, the sick fuck noun you were to me, the viciousness, the depravity, the trembling shaking weeping crying convulsions, the lightheadedness, the loss and absence of breath, the affected British accent – lost when you cursed at me, the duplicitous nature of your words and actions, the hyperventilating, the vomiting, the screaming, the cackle, the rants, the rage, the shrieking leering hovering howling wraith that you had become, the pale other-worldly distant vacant eyes that were now yours

the error you made having mistaken my kindness for weakness,

the night I left you,

sleeping in the airport on New Year's Eve,

the pathetic marriage proposal that you sent me,

the absolute grotesque and unthinkable mendacity of it all.

The Princess of New Julfa

Onyx shining cobra
her mouth to my own

quick
rapid
sharp
strikes

piercing me

mouth to lip to tongue
cheek to neck to chest

she draws
drinks
slakes
and swallows
my blood and breath

depleting and devouring

in the bright to brighter
glowing of my surrender

A Note Found in a Re-used Prescription Bottle

all the beautiful
little
jenny-blue pills are gone

and now
so am I

A Short and Timely Reply

had Prometheus a mirror, what would he have
seen—he saw instead,
along the great and rising reaching walls,
the magnified shadow of self and there ...

had Icarus a mirror, what would he have seen—
he saw instead,
swiftly rushing over crest of water and wave,
the magnified span and shadow of self and then ...

If you had a mirror, you would still be looking into
   it now,
a thoroughly Modern Ms. Narcissus,
having still not realized that I was gone,

had you a mirror, would you ever look into it
   and see the truth?

not who you think you should be;
not who you want others to see you as;
not who you aspire to be

but indeed, what it is that you are?

mirror, mirror on the wall,
Ms. is blind to each and all.

Epilogue: 708-A

"How long have you been holding your breath?
When was the last time your eyes were open?

Do you remember much at all of what happened?"

> "I remember the soft puff and pressure of
> cotton balls on my eyelids while they were
> taped shut
>
> I remember the sounds of the surgical
> instruments being prepared,
> cold quick metal
> the sudden sharp pinch pain
> rising to fade,
> fading to fading,
> as the air turned over and over again on itself
> overwhelmed by the smell of ammonia
>
> I remember when my mouth was opened,
> when the pipes were put down my throat
> the ridged plastic tubes, the taste of chalk
>
> I remember when the pumps were implanted
> the strange sense of unfamiliar cold moving
> clicking, clicking from within

> I remember the sound the Attendant made
> when he first saw my body cleared of bandages
> while he lowered me into the burn bath
> he quick gasped and winced."

"Do you remember how you got here?"

> "Yes, I was playing with matches."

"There were no matches when we found you."

> "What did you find?"

"We found you—alone—she had already left—the door was open"

> "Do you mean that she is gone—she is not coming back?"

"Yes."

> "Do you promise?"

The Blue Morning Kitchen Sessions

When That Time I Saw

eyes sparkle,
smile bright to the moment

above her neck decorated with stones, amber
made precious simply because they are hers
made precious simply by their closeness to her
skin,
neck and body

graceful and flowing brown peasant blouse
complementing her small breasts
her skin the colour of soft cinnamon

woman, a posture of comfort and confidence,
energy and enthusiasm of her voice
telling and reminding of the girl still within

standing close, seeing her in full
she carves, cuts and sculpts denim
her jeans, effortlessly tracing
her lines

auburn curls, soft and flowing,
finger to curl – to gently place a lock
and strand behind her ear
in a polite acknowledgement, she leans
slightly into the space between us
filling our conversation further in the
night air, cooled and salted by the Bay

I hope to see her again
I will look for her
again by the gentle water's edge

Prophecies Foretold Of Her

     I.

songs, poems, myth and fable
legends tell of her

sandal-clad
footprints in the sands of ancient and eternal Egypt

silhouette, statuesque
Sun quenched hair and simple fabric dress
flowing under Sun and Moon
atop outcrop in Delphi
in Meteora
in distant height above the Mediterranean shining
silver
platinum and gem blue

waters endlessly to shore and rocks to stone
  and pebble
as they have through the centuries stretching to
find reach rise and to touch her

in the bazars of Persia
in the Turkish market
among the multitudes
her eyes shining out and of a singular glow

hunched and hushed exchanges that it was indeed
her who was seen

are shared through the patient blue rising writhing
smoke of the hookah

on the glen in Kerry at first light dawn
at dusk along the rising hills of the Wicklow
Mountains among the sweet swaying shadows
above the great waters—the Atlantic—on the Cliffs
of Moher

when with giggle and quick step bounce and
brilliant blur of hair
nimbly dancing barefoot across the Giant's
causeway steps to her familiar
where Cú Chuliann too had walked

shepherd and sailor alike eyes closed breathe
deeply and listen to
and for her song

peeking from a doorway in Quartier Latin
sitting quietly within a garden in Hampstead
moving among the frenzied flock and Manhattan
masses
crossing a street in SoHo
gypsy in jeans
the gentle bell of her jewelry echos

songs poems myths and fable
legends tell of her

II.

I have now seen her
I have been welcomed to her long embrace
I have been gifted the soft and sensual touch of her
elegant fingers and lips to my own
to face mouth body and tongue
I have been drawn within the vast and vibrant
stretching colours and charisma of eyes
bright and radiant with wonder

III.

I share with her

"I have ascended into love with you"
and pause

"Drink deep of me, I have been found."

She whispers in reply

In Wander, Wonder, Wait, And Worship

She asked,
eyes squinting in thoughtful and sincere curiosity
soft smile in compliment

"Where have you been?
Why has it taken so long to find you?"

I replied

"I have been waking before dawn – to know
its warmth and glory
looking West to see its final radiance its final glow
and glimmer before night
surrender

sitting beside the brook watching its mellow
meander and slow patient peaceful glide in
the presence of the perfume of lilies; beside the
seas listening to the pace of waves – lifting and
bowing, rising and falling in grand harmonious
rhythm and scale, enveloped in salt mist and spray

climbing to summit of rock and mountain heights to
breath new, stretching and filling my lungs in the full
and free air of pure wind and Delphinium

sitting, quietly, in worship – in church, and in
temple, in tent and in hut – on pew and on hair, on
rug and dirt – listening to music, song and prayer –
the giving of thanks and the

monastic rhythmic offerings of gratitude within
translucent smoke, of incense, candle and oil

huddling in libraries readying and studying the
scribes, the poets and poetesses – continuing to
open mind, open spirit, open imagination to words,
wonder, cadence and call – soul illumination from
parchment and quill and its craft and gift

taking my body and laying it down beneath the
moons and stars of Copernicus to allow
grandeur and the boundless night sky and obsidian
space to teach me and remind me of humility

It is there that I have been."

"why so long?" she asked

"I needed to see these things – to begin to know
these things – to ensure I recognized each in the
beauty and magnificence, in the gentle design and
shape, in the quiet kindness and care, in the
splendor and grace that is you."

If Sought

when it is that morning
slow
lifts its eyes to you
will you recognize this day
as first
as yours
as new?

you will find me
should you wish
already in the garden

beginning again
the delicate and deliberate
invitation
the patient heart hand work
of seeding

Details

Do you mean like those of the way
you stand in posture with ease
straight tall and perfect petite
in you and in the space of
the blue morning kitchen

hair loose flow curl curly
to and along your shoulders
warm wisp to neck and tuck to ear
robe loose tied to waist,
beneath which those slender
girl got hips,
the glide curve of your flat stomach
the steady certain long lean rise of legs to the
splendor of your gift between

warm cup cradled gently by elegant fingers slow to
lip—mouth and drink sigh

squint smiling with radiant eyes
promise made and delivered

Morning
kiss Dawn delicate fingers pause on cheek hold
kiss breath slow blink eyes again wide the color
 of the Aegean
reminding Dawn that She too must pause,
She too has beauty to witness and behold
while you stand in the blue morning kitchen

if it is those, then "yes," I reply

As I join you,
with cup with boy grin marvel
with you

Desire

do not allow yourself to forget
even for a moment
the slow dance of Desire
when the song of this
our vagabond bard
came into the half light of the living room ballroom

releasing the walls to infinity
stretching the floor and the horizon line
to give and share with you
each precious inch of room
to sway and linger and grace
as it push swept you to my arms

forget not the gentle rhythm that came to you
and that which you so freely welcomed
forgetting altogether a previous confession of
necessity to lead
we danced together then and there
in the gift glow space
in that moment
to music and poetry
intuitively instinctually elementally
known and recognized

from first call note
to and through the final breath sigh echo resonance
from the hot tar of night and Newark
the crumbled cement corners of Brooklyn
the sands of Mozambique

the quiet blue reflections
in the Chelsea Hotel

the wonder waltz of new love promise
powered and purposed
propelled by belief and hope
gift details,
like angel ornaments,
to a new and up reaching tree
of green great glorious growth

visions, like whisper light wings of a Sprite,
as they swirled, whirled
and welcomed us

Indoctrillumination

light of candle bright...
a simple breath
puff delicate
away from darkness

amid blue light soft
of new fire

lick and feather
lifting and floating
from give of sharp tip
pierce and pulse
and soft curve flame

to shadow
and the grand slow unfolding
picture clicking
wake wobble
of and in strobe cadence
delight and dissolve
touching and alive
bathing renewing and reviving
each piece of you
the accessories and acquired objects of your collection
set carefully upon your night dresser

light cast dancing
by each candle newly placed and arranged
waving and weaving

the hymn hum
whisper chorus suggestion
and seed secret
illuminated for the moment
brief bright to eye
obscured quick squint seen
back and again to and between
shadow and shape and shift
hypnotic

the delicate display enthralled entangled enticing
perfume and petals
jewelry and gem stones
oils opiates and the shuttering shadow on and of
the Buddha

I remember wishing in the dreamscape
that you summoned and unveiled

while long and naked and patient and eternal and
standing
you lean
you lady
you lovely

not seen in full however

there surrounded by the lights that you had
conjured
your slender hips set smartly subtly thrust forward

this, while the room exploded and expanded
exponentially
this landscape and legend

latitudes and longitudes lost

as at first and in and through the centuries before this moment
from the crooked heaven pitch precipice placed dome
high above your body and bed

sheets galloping and gliding out and under from beneath us
like ocean and cloud
through the once walls now gone
and lost to ancient and new forest forever

small fire
to you, cousin and kin and clan,
to me, before me, above me, below me, beside me
in again through and as if across the chasm and chaos
this, your ritual made light

the fire that you called and rose and made
in the truest and naked state of you

yet, only through the burn,
my having learned too late,
that this was not a celebration,
but instead,
to signify and begin

the sacrifice

Known Not Sought

dying in the space and pace of sidewalks
enthusiasm and energy depleted lost spilled
on concrete and gravel
alone
staggering pushed
again lost confused in crowds
with heart of gaping hurt and hollow

dying in the shallow breath
once grace – now gone
of mornings no more
of afternoon walks wander and Sun
of night star sky wish sacred Summer mystery
and new air none

dying in each sweet smell of new cut slice ginger
the tease tumble crunch crack of mill grind salt,
pink and pepper
where we dined danced and dared

dying in each dark winged evocation of the angel's note
from cello
deep mystery called and conjured forth
from unseen dark chamber beyond the reach
of candle care and caress

dying quietly in the remote tender snap of tree branch

the whisper drift drop of leaf to still soil and spinning Earth
and sad sail flower petal fall to cool creek and cold current

swift not – but certain death
slow closes the hand casket and curtain

having collected the scorched and scattered scraps
of the shuddering husk of what I had been

I am now past the dying
I am become Death
destroyed of you
you my beautiful never guessed Oppenheimer

The Heart Knew First

    I.

whether by
frostbite
or fright

my fingers and finger tips had turned black

in themselves the black fear
writhing rising raging
pain howl horror and savage

my fingers became black to catch collect the
   pooled poison
to save halt hold this infection
from reaching the silent empty chambers of my
heart

    II.

"We have not yet told the heart that you are gone –
that you have left us.

We are still trying to stop the screaming voices in
the head
and put the hands out – they are still on fire

some of us think that the heart already knows that
you are gone— that

it knew first
and that is why it is silent and gray
having stopped and no longer sending blood."

    III.

the smell of burning flesh was horrible
but who could have imagined

that the smoke would be
so thick
so black
and that there would be so very much of it

The Bounty

the basket
is still there
by the door

my Daughter's
two little dresses
are on the bed

your Son's
new shoes
beside the dresser

my scarf and jacket
upon a chair

your once dress
behind the closet door
slightly ajar

the house is silent

the bounty
there in the basket
made of ten hands and hearts
now spoiled

Fall has come
cruel and certain
and taking and final

sky
warning of cold
and death
and an unattended wake
in Dublin to follow

And So Begins the Folding Down

and so begins the folding down
the necessary delicate work of hands

midmorning hush
house and horizon
and window west

sheets
removed from bed,
washed in care,
dried in light,
folded to corners matching

with hands of ever so slight
light tremble and memory
of that once boundless

fragrant theses
of once Summer
sea and salt, body and breeze, sweet sweat of you
ginger and fig, lilac, licorice and rose

perfumed once, gone now
drawn and released and away from these woven fibers
the steady slow circle
rolling and over and again of cold water cold

blue crisp up sky
slow lap of linen on line
on great green hill of now right round arc and run

ocean and surf down-up below
while the rhythmic reach rise and repose
where yard and hill and sparrow and blue and
August bright last

sheet and wind
in slow dance waving curling
as once we too had in harmony
sweep lift reach linger descend rise again grace low
fade and again

as we had once in the blue morning kitchen
in the soft evening parlor
in the spark-light candle wave shine bedroom

where and as of star and fire too –
grand wide spinning in dizzying dark and sky and
here
where Earth and heart and dream and dance
dissolved

sheets
clean
washed
carried now
no less heavy then Winter's great gray blanket

sheets,
held in final task and turn
carried
where hand and finger to closet door handle,
to lock twist of armoire,
hand slow still flat
now knowingly

steady upon sheet
upon shelf and Summer gone

while, from window,
sought long sought
now needed
brought found
slow and cool
Autumn's first
whisper
wink
hint
call

the great long and slumber
and rest and rise
to now and forever gone Summer

An Account of Her Most Recent Visit

      I.

new Summer new
old Summer old

your gold to bronze
your blue to gray
your twilight to merely shadow

yet still
this very shore of ancient ocean
still whispers and hums
and coos calls beckons

not and no longer to sail
search and sojourn
to find you

that has been done

once and ago
and you yourself can read of my having discovered
you
and you may find
it and other things there still
in the parchment in Greece

instead to push off

deep plunge

azure waves endless
ancient cresting white
and purple

to now and forever leave this wreckage

and concede this once fine ship
to rook and bittern
gull and crab

to wind wave and sand

to leave this wreckage
and sail new again

in a small slender single craft
a fisherman's boat

handmade in the vision, the inspiration
design knowledge and traditions shared
of my outlaw Brothers and Sisters of the fires tents
and shores of Galilee

a boat that once – but needed not but for gift and
grace – and mercy
held the feet of the Wild Christ

and carry on shoulder this boat
across scrub and rock and territories field and dry
to the shore of the Mediterranean chalice
to sail West

II.

sail West
like others of wounds survived
and seeking only Peace

and West
with wind and knowledge made of wounds,
insights cut of scars and seeking wisdom water
wake
and West

wounds, filling the bottom of this small boat, wet
and flopping like a great catch of fish

when air and Sun
begin to harden
before they quiver not again, with eyes open and
light receiving, by hands,
quench them back in the sea

III.

and to rigging adjust
and sure to sail,
and hold
and hand and heart to line
and eyes to horizon widening

sail into the West
voyage new
and wave
and wonder

The East Village Sessions

A Cup of Coffee, A Cigarette
    And An Attempt To Read
        The Day's Newspaper

again the city summer heat leapt and lurched from
sewer drain and subway from corner and curb from
fire escape— where there was none—street tar and
rubber searing up and out of each crack and
crevice while the sweat of strangers passed in drip
smudge and bump from arm and shoulder to arm
and shoulder at corners and in crowds the quick
pace of Manhattan slowed not yet among the
movements there were those whose wasted and
warn wander was visible sticky skin and denim
sundress and shades heat crackle color collage
snaking and twisting whirling and writhing in and
out of avenue sidewalks crowded with shadows
morphed exaggerated elongated gaudy the
grotesque extension of bodies the labored pace of
people wearing laundry white cotton ruined
yellow—the soil of sweat urine yellow cabs darting
as humans dive into the pedestrian surf into the
street from crumbling cement corners breasts
young and old alike, bounce drag or dangle
beneath tee-shirt and peasant blouses the requisite
pack of punkers—walk'n hard talk'n loud and doing
"A"-jack-shit chain smoking and laughing and hiding
loudly in pegged jeans and god-on-fire combat
boots and the march of Brooks Brothers clientele
with suit jacket perfectly poised over a shoulder the
hard heavy procession of the immigrant elderly
women pulling and women pushing small thin
chrome and black wheeled carts to and from the

market and again the Israeli and Persian women
beautiful born of heat and fire cool and graceful and
flowing they alone glide past fast through the
troubled clogged push stop stagger halt begin
again of Manhattan

#6 Uptown Summer

City speak jump and jive
Summer street sing and saunter
Push break dash pause turn
Laugh holler howl giggle sigh "Hey"

Pace up—this day is moving
Hot to Cool
Cocoa later, milky creamy iced coffee pow Now

Clear diamond ice tonic
Gin to the welcome
Soda pop sip
Sweet lips kiss
"Mine Oh Mine Oh Mine"

Shoulders to show
Shades to the glow glare
She is smiling and I am smiling
And I'm not even there yet

Summer: Downtown #2

kick crawl
shudder stop
loco

beneath her skin
below her face
made garish

by lights
too many

and the mad
sad rising
of too many folk flies

the silver in her veins

past pass passenger
reeling reaching screeching to South Ferry
beyond to someone else's Far Rockaway
to where she not waits
any linger longer
lone long ago
lost gone
girl

E. H. Sailing – 1911

sails
ironed up
by wind and light

to eye and sky
snap bright
rise in crisp first reach
meeting bird and wing
and want above

grace flutter
turn and to turn
cut and coast and rise and fall ins steady measure
maritime rhythm
up and after to meet again
bow nod stay
wink play push
and forward and side and about and more

tac-tac-tac-tac-tac
tie and release
draw good quick
release
let
hold and lean
let and rise up and up
over and to
the new weight and touch density of wet white rope

pace rise quick above near flight bound and grim
holding steady

heart race
still holding like some smarter cousin of Icarus

sails up
warm and wind filled snap taut
caught in heat up lift
crisp cutting into the modern moving blue

from air above
push down
while the drop plane horizon suddenly there
and below and now overhead
of boat

grand gush moment
of water and white and froth and throw
and moments
and movement of this fast flashing

when wind lift wind in top of wind
up down
all wind now in full to the sailor
eyes wide in wonder and humble piety

sharp cut sharp into sky
split steering streaming glimmer gleam on water

rough high
pushed low
thrust ahead again and forward
deep still and too and vessel
sheering across the deep
always water

sharp cut sharp cast
in the sky these sails bright still
to bright

face sunned
mouth wet of splash jump of sea and salt
body jolt
wet colder still that seasons ago once Winter's
window breath
holding suspended yours now
the sea in its forever drum cold reverberation o
depth

pulled and pushed
to deepen deeper
into the magnificent ancient body deep

The White Horse
    (New Amsterdam on Hudson)

    I.

this
the olde cold
of sooty gray London
here too
in
the still young
rising timber smoke
of New Amsterdam
where
shadow and shade
grin in wicked macabre
October delight
cold
as sky
slouched from river east
where
big-hearted bright
not close enough hearth
and Hudson to the near west
cold still
enough to wet sweater
chill skin thin
in shiver silent shake
cool of bone
deep and within

II.

proper pints poured and spilled glisten
atop this oblong box
a toast—still is echoes
where there are many
and you
young wild curled haired boy
Thomas
never doubting
poor lad
they bent not to genuflect
not to tie the laces of their shoes
should they be so fortunate
not to strap their boots better still
if they were blessed with work
no
young darling boy
this beautiful Thomas
they crouched in unison to
the foot rail
ready and waiting and worn
your bearers
to carry you.

III.

some find it odd and some disturbing
that I weep here
I find it sad
the familiar melancholy
of Autumn
stained again
in colors up bright

punching the sky
before dizzy daze
pause
and drifting
I do so alone
I find it so very sad
and that they
no longer

The Studio Sessions

Why whisper

"Why whisper" she asked
shoulders set
prepared to ponder
in proud polite poised posture

head tilted
girl curiosity intact
soft gentle—modest still
in the bright sparkle of question
and moment of new-eyed possibility

"because it allows for me to lean in
lean into the space between us
and slowly

while asking…

will you greet accept and welcome me to your ear
and imagination?

while filling my eyes
with the rich radiance of yours
deep hued and almond

closer to see in slow motion slow
the blink from nearly but just a lash away

providing the full fill of lungs
with the rich bouquet of your thick luxuriant
  warm rose hair

as my mouth moves closer to your ear
to ensure that no single word
single beat
single syllable
is spilled dropped or lost

reaching deep into that grand hair flow
flowing to shoulder
and to sensual slender on high neck
needing no decoration
but for my mouth and lips and tracing fingers

when too and still and next whisper met and made
your eyes evoked wide wonderment
delight of new surprise
body and lungs—yours—now filled again
now with new air new again
as your beautiful Summer ripened Sun
made brown breasts rise

posture responding in full
needing as you and responding as you do will may
   wish must
by intrigue and instinct

while slim waist hips
soft curves of you
tenderly twitch in this state of anticipation
   and allure

while still the beautiful brown petite belly trembles
stomach muscles quick flinch within
sudden flash body pulse wonder

and warmth
rise from there your beautiful treat treasure
secret of you."

Why To Have Paused?

Why to have paused?

for only in having done so
would I have come to know these things

by temporary oasis
reflection and repose

should I have only looked ahead
should I never have stopped moving forward
should I have never left from where it was that I
was before
and begun
to travel
wonder
wander
journey

what then of this?

I would not have found
this gentle nestled treasure
among the landscape of time
swirl and sand

here
where light for eyes
tree for shade
ground for feet
water for quench

food for body
quiet for head health and healing
touch of hand and heart

was shared

compassion
and gratitude
passion
purpose

and prayer
whether said aloud
or to self
said in whisper
or in song
said in private
or in practice

like the young Andalusian shepherd
once thought lost

journey
seek and find he did

thoughtful
and thought thorough

pause
and poised
purposed and pointing

yet never and not by standing still

Once a Hummingbird: Again A Flower

The hummingbird glowed
ecstatic
drinking deeply from the new-found flower

the flower unfolded itself
blushed
whispered
"drink, drink, drink"

the hummingbird
eyes closed
breathed
drank again and ascended

the flower
having given what it is that it gave
lifted itself
as it has done before
to the bird

On the Celebration of Your Entrance
And Unveiling

I.

in the quiet of the studio lit by natural light
a dancer floats before the mirror

with purposeful eye
to watch
to study
to gift

her movements with elegance and grace designed

in the presence of two truths

II.

in the quiet of the studio lit by natural light
an artist reaches to a canvas

with purposeful eye
to see
to examine
to gift

her colors shapes and gentle strokes
stepping back from the canvas to receive again the
beauty

in the presence of two truths

III.

born are the artists
architects actors writers
poets dancers and painters
alike

compelled to seek
search and realize
however

briefly

the temporary beauty
and symmetry of nature's lines

The Embrace

Have you begun to count the brushstrokes
of the Mad Master of the Robe?

have you begun to catalog and curate
each colour he has gift cast before you?

have you shuddered?

breath lost realizing the impossible truth of it …
that he understood had been there was personal witness
that his images are of you

toes form feet to push lift and steady
fingers form hands stretch to touch hold

in his precision
the absolute greatest reach of our bodies
our selves our beings

reaching
finding
and surrender

I saw the brushstrokes

I trembled and wept in ascending joy and love

then
and once

cradling now only the image
and gazing upon the brushstrokes

then and only then
once and only once
I thank the master for remembering

it is my treasure
my torment

Poem In G Minor

      I.

I am not sure
that it might not be best for both
that I get dressed
and
go

I am not sure that you understand

what you thought you heard
when you watched my lips
while you again heard
only your wish want words

instead of the terrible truth
that I shared

      II.

truth of
the severe
severed and stilted limits
of my heart

boundaries too narrow
reach inadequate
pulse too shallow
pain too deep

heart skin black and revolting
rolling over and over and over again upon itself
becoming slow thicker and hardening

until the near drop stop

dead

    III.

there
it is done
said again

    IV.

I surrendered

not to love or trust or faith
not to forgiveness or grace
not to the redemptive power of the Blood of Christ
the tears of Mary
the kind hands of Joseph

I surrendered
not to patience
or prayer
or Providence

I surrendered not to you
or this
or anything else here shared wished or imagined

I surrendered

back there
back then
to her

I surrendered to her
her and her alone

      V.

and I am still there

      VI.

broken and deformed
in grotesque genuflection

Still Life (Now Properly Titled)

we were sitting in your beautiful home
in your warm living room
surrounded by the delicate details of you
and paintings of flowers lighted by your hand

we laughed heartily
warmly wonderfully
together so very often

we argued rarely and then
only of worthy things

though when we did you became less precise
sloppy even
your words rattled by frustration
were less well chosen

costly and caustic to the ear they fell upon

my own

they failed to match the rest of you

The North Beach Sessions

The BEAT

you can hear it somewhere out there above
beneath beyond the BEAT near flash-pan Mardi-
Gras horns ripping the purple night shredding the
curtains letting the window wide wind in, in and in
close to the doum-ddooum-ddoouumm doum-
ddooum-ddoouumm Ddooomm Dmm Duddumm
Dun-Dun-Dun-Dum-Dummmmnnn Of the big man
bass fully erect yet leaning back like some tea'd out
cat still stretching reverberating in wisdom
drenched laughter Sneaking up from beneath the
rattlesnake on fire writhing atop the snare drum
while the cobra call hiss hiss shhh shhh shh of the
cymbal brushes glide still lightly and light beside the
tap-tap-che of pop top high-hat certain and neat
and near perfect a punctuation exclamation right in
the middle of the phrase connecting Almost in the
keys man glistening gliding riding over top and tip
toe like the feet of Fred Astaire up and down the
white and black steps the brush just touch like
feather sweep sweet side-to-side sway Gene Kelly
from side-to-side when then and there beneath the
stomp to pedal and hold pause hold repose and
pop again finger water rain on the little keys to this
kingdom On this piano – too big to get in the gin
joint and up these stairs "How the hell are we all
gonna fit on that little stage in that corner?" with the
beautiful shine like onyx "Baby-baby it's you – it's
beautiful you" singing baby grand Somewhere
behind the beat somewhere there in a single note a
voice that brought it all – whisper, sometimes howl

"Alive she cried." we was together and the beat took all the trouble and like a child threw it into the air like confetti for us to scramble up and tease a tune night after frightful and dangerous blues jazz night "Round and round it goes – where it stops? Shit – we knew that too?" Right here again at the bottom beginning of it all the last place that light and color was seen and we – mad driven in the scene – scramble down the rabbit hole chasing a hare in a waistcoat with pocket watch – like a hipster pimp with feet too big for spats – and a young blonde girl with dress the color of sun-lit lavender dream, still dreamin' one big within a dream

Who's That With The Horn?

"Hey, who's that? Who's that cat with the horn?"

"Who is that, you ask…
Who's kinda blue in kinda royal purple? Huh?
Huh, who, on the corner—right there right now right close
not but a blink away
like the sky so wide open
ever expanding expansive standing commanding

Who? Who is that studying it all, man?
Standing head up
and down
Beat up
beat down
beat-to-beat
beat-iful!!!!

Smiling anywhere everywhere behind that
The good silver cup chalice
Poured shared and sure—yeah!

Who the hell is that zip-krak-cat
all lit up and in the middle of it all
– the center of it all
– how now and it and all
takin' tokin' snakin' smokin'
givin' gettin' lookin' leerin' leanin'
and lift leavin' the scene

and the ground
without even moving his feet

Who, in that just right night tight silent way
in person
in tune
instrumental
insatiable
indescribable
instantaneous
and Immortal

close and closer still yet
the outreaching magnificence
Oracle and Seer
Shaman and Sage
Martyr and Mystic
Music-man and Muse
On wind and black hawk wing

That man, that man there, must have listened to
everything—body and note;
heard everything—body and note
needed to follow no one—chose to findfollowfind
the beat the good beat the new beat
THE BEAT

He is it – Kat Crème Brûlée"
Rip Tip of the Tip Top Pop Top

Slow out!
Gone man gone!!

in some smoke blue in milk with silver streamers

ascended surrender bow when he slowly lowered
his head over his horn
like Buddha in cheshire grin jazz club corner trio
Come up and eyes wild new bright radiant

He was in the horn now and the horn was in him
and the beat, THE BEAT had them both
the beat was playing through his blood bones lungs
lips fingers in uninterrupted lines
with that silver wand magic wind machine

White
Black
Silver
Blue
Mace
Magik

That, who is that? Who is that cat with the horn?
Who is that?

That baby, that baby is Miles, baby—Miles.

That young'un is Mr. Miles Davis

Miles 'muthafuckin' Davis

Pied Piper of the night delight

Be careful now—He knows All about it …

Did You See Her?

Did you see Her?
She was right here
floating
above the bed
watching you sleep

She came last night
it was late I guess
I had been up still working

you were lying there sleeping
your soft-away breath
the only sound before Her arrival
in the black silk silver silence

She came right through the ceiling
and was right bright beautiful above you

the ceiling itself shimmered
  and gleamed
and pulsed and waved
and turned into water
glistening
suspended
inverted up above you

and in that moment
emerging

She descended

delicately down
came gently over you
hovering just above your body

I thought that Her hair
or robe
or wings
were going to tease touch tickle your face
  or body

Her fingers were long and lighted
and slowly and with abundant care
traced and twinkled over each detail of you
like a fantastic fast field of butterfly wands
  of magic
giving and receiving
recognizing and renewing
in gift and good and grace

I for a brief second
in honor of this Holy Magic Cosmic
  Cradle Kiss
began to weep and wonder if it was possible
was it real?

Could She really be there
and you there
and me there
and Her floating like that?

what was it that I was seeing
  and hearing and feeling?

the breeze whisper to cheek of soft
   feathers wings winking slowly
as if they were themselves
submerged in a clear crystal
liquid diamond of light flowing

yeah, I knew it was real
knew that it was real
and so many things
there and then
too came forward again
and showed themselves to be real

my eyes while dizzy wide wandering
glazed across the mirror
there along the wall
was She there too?

She was there yes
and radiant

She still is—come here
take a close look at this thing now

do you see that?
radiant out shimmer light burst subtle
   illuminated warm brush strokes of light
Her wings
somehow and now permanent

on this mirror
lens
window

as if a photograph negative
light made imprint of the impossible
that had just happened
to each of us

I wonder if She'll be back?

I got the distinct impression last night
that this was not the first time
She had come to watch you

Do You Dare?

       I.

do you dare?

remove
your velvet hat
blossomed with embroidered rose

gently, yet purposefully
push aside your intentional
and thought necessary bangs

locks the colour to match
the flower above,
so as not to hide your eyes
obscure your vision

So that you can best see
that which is before you
as it truly is

not of sideward
glance or squint
but centered with clarity

this beautiful vessel of you
petite and wondrous,
graceful in contour
of lines smooth
and uninterrupted

yet, still only filled
a bitter
and emboldened,
crested and corked
bottle of smoke

it will fail you

as poison
and potions do,
again and again,
unfair and unkind

neither whisper nor want,
nor worry
will empty this thing made

will
and will alone
may allow in time
new wine
of vine ancient and eternal,
rooted and reaching,
in slow stretching twist to light

to fill and overflow
this new-claimed chalice
of your own divinity

II.

with hands steady
unstitch the flower from your hat
hold it within your hands
and before your heart

bare witness
The Rose of Jericho

Midsummer's Knight, Dreams

I.

gentle doth light fall
in Summer's Sweet Surrender

to window wished once
echo
near not far

has this day been gifted
sufficient lived resolve
will wait of moon
or rose repose
repose?

Surely not
When tenant's up
Bard and Bacchus to apron thrown

II.

sweet ears to candy
Muse
be devil or delight

clever feather
bright you are
of morning day and strife

known to me
must you be
your promised
plundered night

Wish Me Something New

      I.

wish me something new

whether you be gypsy, conjurer
necromancer or genie

I have found only bottles empty
bones shattered
cloth torn tattered

and ghosts
in whisper and wander

no treasure for the young Andalusian shepherd boy
no fleece of gold for the Son of Iolkos

only salt and Sun and sea-worn Odysseus

      II.

I find Prometheus

Newly blinded and bound

Not to mountainside
But instead

To Sisyphus's cruel stone

On Russian Hill

      I.

there you find yourself

yourself
if you know to know

there again
beneath the new chrome metallic glistening night
breathing
healing
heaven
whisper and wishing

rubbing your hands together near the trash can fire
quick to coat pockets a Chesterfield and a Zippo
a favorite gift to you from you to you from then
of once ago pawn shop
if you had only been James and knew who
   Uncle Benny was
and why congratulations were in order years
and years and years ago
wondering again about them now

you offer and share a smoke with the new old new
old always friends
brothers and sisters
listening to the pop-fizz-crackit-spurff-sssnap
   as wood shatters
burning within the trashcan

casting hurling – birthing new stars straight
   and sometimes sideways up and out
to brief fly flight
and exhaust on sidewalk, collar
   and cuff of this
this little huddled new-made tribe

      II.

two bottles pass around
arriving to you at the same time
rare
the wine is Red Red Red Rioja and Malbec

you slug and pull from one and then the other
as new wine is made there in your mouth
across your lips and tongue and throat
and warm deep deep
while spilling just a bit
laughing
not alone
and more laughter
passing with joy and certain generous grateful
   hold hand
pass to another each other

sharing
folks just wanting to stand a little closer
hug and kiss a little longer

as night drapes
drenches and drinks us
christening and anointing each

in
silver
platinum
perfection

above apricot and wild-rose-colored fire
made in tribute

and soon and so and so

      III.

are you in the Bronx tonight, sleeping in Spanish
Harlem, Sunnyside – maybe?
down on Astoria Boulevard, the East Side or
praying away in Camden

Or have you flown flew further West still
and again Chicago, again East St. Louis or again
there rising on the mountain
on that great gray and green garbed Denver?

have you laid your blanket down in the Mission are
you there in Fillmore?

Just look 'a ways up

North

Do you see that new fire?

We are waiting for you on Russian Hill

and no one is going anywhere

until you and Dawn breathes please kiss us

not goodbye
not so long
but only good God Gaia morning

and then we'll wander down to along the wharf
and find coffee
and share read the newspaper together

quiet and in Love
each one of us with the other

and know this

About the Author:

John J. McKenna is a New York-born, Princeton-based writer, whose efforts range from poetry and longer prose to academic studies. John is a grateful member of the New Hope Beat Poets Society (New Hope, PA). John's inspiration – beyond the visits of myriad Muses (some of darker voice & wing than others) – flows from Rumi, Emerson and Whitman through Ginsberg, Jack K. and Bukowski to current torchbearers – flamethrowers hell raisers like Kim Addonizio. John believes in wine, women and song. John's poetry has appeared in The River Poets Journal (Editor: Judith Lawrence) and Vox Poetica (Editor: Annmarie Lockhart).

www.JohnjMcKenna.net

Artist's Biography:

Marissa Woodrow is a print-maker, drafts-woman, photographer, model, and seeker. With West Coast roots, and a BFA in Printmaking from San Francisco's Academy of Art University, Marissa now lives and works on the east coast.

Her images merge a romance between photography, portraits, and the graphic qualities of printmaking, in order to document an emotional running narrative. Traditionalism, and the appreciation for archaic processes funds a healthy hunger to move from the heart, to the mind's eye to the hand with focus. Although she has been trained in several traditional mediums (i.e. oils, sculpture, and primarily printmaking), her more recent work is in creating narrative diptychs through digital photography.

Marissa Woodrow's work has been shown cross-country, and resides in personal collections, as well as on commissioned posters, album art & T-shirts. Her career in the arts extends beyond the purely creative. She has been active in printmaking/art instruction, artist talks, and curating.

www.reddashboard.com

Made in the USA
Middletown, DE
04 November 2016